I Spend So Long Evaporating

poems by

Rebecca Kositzke

Finishing Line Press
Georgetown, Kentucky

I Spend So Long Evaporating

Copyright © 2025 by Rebecca Kositzke
ISBN 979-8-88838-890-7 First Edition
All rights reserved under International and Pan-American Copyright Conventions. No part of this book may be reproduced in any manner whatsoever without written permission from the publisher, except in the case of brief quotations embodied in critical articles and reviews.

Publisher: Leah Huete de Maines
Editor: Christen Kincaid
Cover Art: Joze Groselj
Author Photo: Katherine Kositzke
Order online: www.finishinglinepress.com
also available on amazon.com

Author inquiries and mail orders:
Finishing Line Press
PO Box 1626
Georgetown, Kentucky 40324
USA

Contents

Introduction xi
What Do You See? 1

One
Brief Enchantment 5
Eventide 6
In a Moment, Everything Can 7
Book Keeper 8
(10 P.M.) Serenade 9
Shooting Stars Only Come When No One's Looking 10
Sanctuaries of Cotton and Electricity 11
Night Vision 12
Due North 13
Advisory 14
Standard Procedure 15
Current 16
Niagara 17
In Anxious Descent 18

Two
Letter to a Pupil 21
At 3 AM, I Am Wolf 22
Art of Freezing 23
Another Tuesday 24
When Ink Doesn't Speak 26
Art of Burning 27
Sometimes I Wonder Why It Has to Rain 28
Photograph Behind the Lids 29
Thirst 30
Illusion 31
Practicing Darkness 32

Three
Night Raid 35
When I Admitted I Didn't Want to Move Fast 36
The Belief of Fictitious Doubts 37
You Wish on Lanterns, I Wish to Be a Lantern 38
In This Mirror 39

To Be a Beast is to Be a Self 40
Spreading Ashes 41
Plunging Vessels 42
X 43
I Am a Neap Tide 44
Don't—Come Find Me 45

Four
Perceiving Obscurity 49
Storm-gazing 50
Afterglow 51
Fuse 52
Nocturnal 53
Castaway 54
Bordering 55
6 A.M. 56
Somewhere Between the Dew and 10 AM 57

End Notes 59
Acknowledgments 61
About the Author 63

In loving memory of Flora Kositzke

Introduction

Emily Dickinson once said, "If I read a book and it makes my body so cold no fire can warm me I know *that* is poetry. If I feel physically as if the top of my head were taken off, I know *that* is poetry. These are the only ways I know it. Is there any other way?"[1] When I made the decision to focus a collection of poetry on my eye disease, Aniridia, I knew I wanted the book to become my struggle, not my blindness. I wanted it to exist as a journey from the protection of light to the hopelessness of darkness. I wanted the reader to feel the darkness closing in.

It may seem cliché to use the concept of light or darkness to describe blindness, but it's because these two things exist so heavily in the life of a blind person. I started asking myself if it was too cliche to use the sunset as a metaphor for vision loss, or to use bioluminescence to reference the struggle of finding light within the dark. That is when I realized the light and darkness *were* my struggle. Aniridia causes a lack of an iris, so the eye cannot regulate how much light goes in. The eyes are sensitive to light, and eventually the disease can lead to complete vision loss. The light and dark weren't just there because we think about darkness when we think of blindness, but because it's *what* I was experiencing. I knew I wanted to portray that in my poems as well. I didn't want to just let the poems talk about water, a mirror, or fireflies, I wanted the poems to experience the hope of catching a firefly, or the fear of unknown, dark waters. I began asking myself questions. Is this poem hopeful? Does it feel hopeless? Is it clinging to the light because night is approaching or because it fears darkness? I began making connections. If the speaker in my poem is trying to hold on to the nostalgia of catching fireflies, the speaker is also afraid of darkness and trying to hold on to hope. That is the experience I wanted to leave in my poems, to move from somewhere hopeful and let the reader sense the hopelessness.

Most of the poems in my collection do not directly mention my blindness, but there are a handful that do. I wrote most of them before I even started making connections to the light and darkness within my writing. These "blind" poems rely more on the experience of blindness, they rely more on the senses. I did want the reader to experience these moments without seeing them, because it is important to grasp the fog or the desire to run from the dark. I have read several books on disability poetry. St. Michaels's Fall by Raymond Luczak or Flare by Camisha Jones provide an idea of deafness. In some cases, the poems let the reader become deaf. I wanted the reader to be on that journey of blindness as well, but I did not want it to be the only thing that existed. Of course, blindness is there, and it is obvious, but it moves in between nature and struggle. This, I feel, allows the poems to become less about blindness and more about the battle with the oncoming darkness: the sunset, the candlelight, the moonlight. The speaker must learn to let go of insecurity and to accept the inevitable. This is why the collection moves through space and time the way it does. It begins at sunset and moves through the night. This, not only implies that things get darker and more empty, but it moves toward the sunrise, a place of acceptance. I know that I will never be able to fully accept my fate, but I try, and that was a large part of my growing process. I had to let go of insecurity and learn to experience the world in a new way. This is also why the collection moves from summer, through winter, and into spring. It moves from a place of comfort to a cold dark space, and back toward a new beginning.

So how can a reader experience blindness when they've only ever closed their eyes to temporary darkness? Matthew Zapruder, in his book, *Why Poetry*, states, "The poem makes this happen for us by placing our mind as we read or listen in consonance with the associations being made by the poem, its 'discoveries, connections, glimmers of expression'... it distinguishes poetry from other forms of writing, not by any particular formal quality—-like rhyme, or line breaks, or musicality, or the use of imagery or metaphor—but by its *effect*." [3] My poems carry a very nostalgic feeling to them, catching fireflies, bonfires on a beach, or even visiting Niagara Falls. In my relationship with viewing the world, I am in a constant state of letting go. Some days it's accepting that something is blurrier than it was a year ago or accepting that the print in a favorite book is too small to read. Because of this, part of understanding vision loss is also understanding that there is always going to be a hint of nostalgia for the things you used to see. Many of those memories came from a time when I was younger, and my vision was better than it is now. It's also learning to experience the world in new ways, as you must let go of your old habits. It's experiencing the world, and then experiencing it all over again, but differently. Experience is a huge part of allowing the reader into a poem. A poet, not only wants the reader to understand the poem, but to *feel* it. The nostalgia for light and the struggle to move forward in darkness are the two things I want the reader to feel most in this, and that is why the fireflies and the extinguished fires are so important. If a reader can understand how much they long for summer in the cold, dark winter months, they can get a hint of what that hopelessness feels like, temporarily.

Simile and metaphor are the best tools for a reader to step inside the speaker's mind, especially on a topic they can't understand. This is why I began to weave nature into the picture. The irises mentioned are, mostly, referring to a flower when the poem is not speaking about a flower at all, but rather the iris of an eye. The sunset was the fading light of vision loss, or the bioluminescence was the tiny hope left within mental and physical darkness. This can also be said for the night or the fog. That is what my future is heading toward, just as it moves toward it in the manuscript. I feel that using nature allows blindness to exist a bit more subtly. I have also found that this exists within the personification of nature. There are many poems within the manuscript that let nature do the talking, or at least speak directly to it, such as talking to Niagara Falls or the fire that is burning itself out. It lets those things become less of a metaphor for dying light and *be* the light. By doing this, It allows, for example, the fog within my manuscript to be something real and tangible. Emily Nilsen has a section of poems in her book, *Otolith*, titled "And What Of the Fog?" As a response, her two, or three, line poems simply give the answer. "Be kind. It only wants to be held" "No use laying traps. It will find a way in and out" "It wants us to stay"[2] In every one of these, Nilsen leaves the reader wanting to know more. Why does the fog want us to stay? Why have we never considered that fog wants to be held? Why does it want to be held? These questions make the fog feel real.

    I feel that most of the manuscript is a conversation between the speaker and the struggle. There's a level of curiosity that slips in for the speaker as well. How did I fit into the world when I wasn't good enough and how am I going to fit in now that I know I cannot be good enough? Who am I in the midst of a sinking ship? Who am I when the moon turns full, and I am sensitive to even dim light? Who am I when raging fires burn themselves out? It is important for the speaker to appear human because, at the end of all our struggles, that is all any of us are. We learn from struggle, we adapt, we grow. So much of my experience on my journey to blindness was self-discovery. That is one of the most important things I have taken away from reading poetry and creating my own story through poetry. It's messy, difficult, personal, and incredibly human. If a poem does not carry ideas, it does not carry experience or emotion either. The first day I started piecing this collection of poems together, I read this quote, "Writing a poem is not so very different from digging a hole. It is work. You try to learn what you can from other holes and the people who dig before you. The difficulty comes from people who do not dig or spend time in holes thinking the holes ought not to be so wet, or dark, or full of worms. 'Why is your hole not lined with light?' Sir, it is a hole."[3] This was fitting, not only in terms of light and dark, but in the humanity and messy emotion of what my experiences mean. There is no way to write about blindness without it getting dark, and there's no way to be that personal without getting messy. The only way to share my experiences with a reader is to let them see the deepest parts of my darkness.

What Do You See?

E

is the hope

the girl clings

to like the fog

latching itself to a freshly

paved road for fear it will dissipate

but the girl still disappears she can't find the road

she's afraid she won't remember how yellow

paints the lanes just like her eyes

won't remember

how to navigate

the letter

E

One

Brief Enchantment

I witness green surrender to my fist
how much life must succumb before
twilight blindfolds itself around us

is it wrong to imprison
fireflies if we set them
free before the hint of dawn

if the humans ask, we'll claim that we're afraid
of a life without the moon, and that these
lanterns are meant to mirror satellites

Eventide

waiting for the darkness to settle
is like begging summer
to promise orange for a few
spare minutes

still, after June
we must accept
of the sun
its fading

In a Moment, Everything Can

we so desperately want to lose our toes
in the white caps— to forget the bonfires behind

(one) *moment*

flickering like insects as we are
crushed by the milky way looming over

(all we have is) *this moment*

a quiet beach overrun by the clashing
of a future where we believe

(we are) *enough*

we are bigger than the grains
beneath our feet

(we are) *not enough to be*

stronger than the dying torches that still
burn before our doubtful eyes

Book Keeper

keep me like a library

hold me delicately in the palms of your calloused hands
as if you fear my spine will break if I bend

treat my skin as if it would tear with every turn of a page

read me read me read me again until you learn
every inch of my dry skin

bandage these paper cuts that slice too deep

don't go too long without dusting these hands in your gentle embrace

I'm susceptible to the quiet space of this worn out carpet
like the dusted yellow pages on the top of shelves

ignite me with the gentleness of a flashlight
left for you inside these fort blankets

whatever you do, never ignite me with the fragile
glow of a flame for libraries can burn faster
than I can call your name

(10 P.M.) Serenade

I wish I could be
this bird, who does not
care the world is
sleeping or the sky
is still
layered in
clouds, this bird
doesn't care if
no one sees
her in the
tops of trees

she doesn't sing
for attention
but for the people
who are too cautious
to leave
their homes. she sings
for abandoned
streets and porch-lit
doorways
she echoes
through
the mourning hours
hoping her voice
will be
the sunrise

Shooting Stars Only Come When No One's Looking

I am foolish
for trusting you to guide me
beyond the frost-
covered swings, waiting

for riverboats to slice their way
through still waters, as we
tangle our hats and scarves
in a heap on the ground

we wait with the river
as we gaze for party lights
like we gaze for constellations

before we leave, you remind me
that all currents lead to
larger bodies of uncertainty

after, we leave, I keep
gazing
after we leave, you keep
swimming

Sanctuaries of Cotton and Electricity

I give up my nightlight the day
my sister moves out
of my room

I convince myself
the monsters move out too
so I leave
the bathroom light
on instead

but monsters begin crawling
along walls, and I tuck
my head under blankets

it is better
to bury myself
where I can't see
the truth as reflected
artificial yellow

that's where the sheets become
colder and the shadows
grow stronger

like autumn does after
the red leaves begin
to dissipate
and I begin to dissipate
the illusion of monsters

    sometimes I still ask the bathroom light
    if it will accompany me to bed
    I ask it to lie beside me and create

    ripples in the sheets so I can pretend
    this sunken mattress isn't only
    sculpted to the form of myself

Night Vision

here, beneath the den of worn out blankets
and expectations
we twirl our useless fingers around
anxious thread
try to count the monsters clawing
at the carpet
always we wait for someone to realize
we are missing
wait while we grow tired of expecting
the sun

here, we still find ourselves

Due North

I don't know why I don't spend more
time looking. I don't know
why green can't exist beyond this frozen

Borealis that arctics itself around
me. I don't know why I can't feel
as significant as the tiny suns that burn

so far away. we give stars so much
credit for looking so small
while I give all my strength

to be like Aurora, I spread myself
thin, and spend my days trying
to collect green circles, but the atoms

that try the hardest are always the ones
that get the least amount of credit

Advisory

white dust hides the flaws of the ground
and birds can't land on bare limbs
frozen sighs can't seep into these cracked walls

this room turns so numb, I can't
reach the windows and doors. frostbite trips
my feet and begs me to stay

my ears forget the sound of breath
but I can still see it fogging
against this bitter air

I insulate myself with loose-threaded
blankets, imagine a warm cup of tea. I make
myself promises I'm too afraid to keep

somewhere between the dying sunlight
and expectations of tomorrow
silence thaws the whispers of snowflakes

Standard Procedure

Decorations assemble in a blur, strands of yellow and red, but as I close my left eye, this triangle is lit on fire by nothing more than a haze of pink. The doctor said in the morning he'd remove the cataract, but stakes are high, and I'm afraid he'll take away more. This haunting tint might be the last thing this eye ever sees. No more surprise on their faces at the pile of presents. No more hunger from the spread of a feast. No more photographs that appear like the white and black from a storm that came just a little too fast. Reindeer-covered houses will slip away as silently as a car clinging to an ice-stricken highway. And if I can't see the pink sky reflecting a fresh snow, I'm not sure I'm willing to let go of a burning Christmas tree.

Current

the blinking yellow where
road meets road
won't change for anyone but the damage
      of wind

how can we, at the edge of
this cliff
expect to walk
away from the whitecaps
      that drown us most

Niagara

I try so hard to believe in the artificial
green they use to illuminate you
but I know it will fall
back into Erie and be stolen
by the current moonlight

In Anxious Descent

I'm afraid of the edge
of the stairs: where I reach
the top and pavement sinks to lower
pavement and my foot searches
                                    disappears

like a box
strapped to a cable, in the face
of a doorway, deciding to
                                    let go

like a boat
that has already shrunk
against the horizon, and continues
shrinking beneath the shoreline
                                    sinking

but I'm not afraid of flying
by day, and especially, by night
for there's something oddly
familiar about the ground

slipping
                                            away

Two

Letter to a Pupil

I wish you would let me believe that my eyes glow like the gentle grass that awakens after the first few rains of spring. I wish you would let me believe they were soft, like the comfort of an old pair of blue jeans, or their brown hue is as warm and sweet as the chocolate drizzled over a sundae.

I wish you would let me believe I didn't have to run from myself. I wish I didn't find myself shaking, as I cower from the switch beside me. I wish the bathroom light was still a comfort to me. I wish I wasn't afraid to look in the mirror after the shower and realize that its shyness doesn't change me. I wish I didn't have to spend forever consumed by this glass casket.

At 3 AM, I Am Wolf

this new moon cuts its way through
the blinds, dipping its toes
in the carpet on the floor

and finds me cowering
at the foot of my bed, trying
to curl beneath the mattress

I am not enough
for the waxing crescent
trying to smoothly reflect

so I deflect, for I know
I will never be as full

these blinds have become bars
these windows feel too small

and hope in these eyes can only
reflect a waning crescent

Art of Freezing

I am a painting of *goodbye*
and I told you so

I am frozen to the nerve-numbing pavement
unable to breathe beneath layers of bounded water

where the air is winter, and bending
power lines and fallen trees

where the atmosphere reflects a pink
blanket caressing the sleeping grass

and the soft pitter patter of falling December kisses
the surface of the months that have gone on before

and I am bundled in my favorite white coat
tears on my face unmoving

as am I, like a deer
in your bright…. dimming… horizon of headlights

all is quiet, not a whisper to be
heard, not the hum of heaters, not even car horns

only the gentle nudge of human
silence against my heavy, jagged breath

Another Tuesday

there's something
daunting
about the actions
I take each night
in attempt to close
my eyes
sitting here with a cup
of decaf coffee
most likely
with cinnamon
toast creamer
in my favorite
new england
mug with a book
of poetry
that tells
a catalog
of unabashed
gratitude
and my gratitude
is only for
this cup of
coffee
and for ross gay
and for my cat
that sits in the window
behind me
waiting for something
to stir
like I wait
and wait
until I force
myself off
the couch
to let go
of unabashed
poetry
and fall asleep
but sleep doesn't

come
because it means

waking up to
another
foggy morning
that returns
and returns
like a line
of poetry
or this mourning
dove
that won't
stop
cooing

When Ink Doesn't Speak

These fingertips graze the beautiful collection of book spines, the way these eyes graze the last ounce of yellow from a dying horizon. The way purples paint the clouds, and purple irises brush the fields, and these fingers brush their way from hard to soft to paper. These fingertips pull out a book they have opened a dozen times, kissing the coarse gentleness of dry pages like the last kiss of a first love

These eyes try to kidnap the ink trapped within

 but these pages weigh more than the heart trapped within

these pages try to memorize what it feels like to be read

until eyes echo the blank these pages bleed

Art of Burning

I associate you as the wildfire
that seeps into my blood and singes
every cell in my body, beautifully

after the day you decide there isn't room
for me, I sit in this old, wooden chair
and paint a picture with poetry

it includes you and it portrays
me, in a room of memory

the chair is on fire

and table legs are kissed by fire
and the frames on the walls are drawn by fire
and our limbs are caressed by fire
and the fear of fire

I can't look beyond the end
of my eyelids—afraid to
find my world disintegrated

I cower from the match
that you ignited
as you smother it
in the depth of my pocket

as you kiss me fiercely
with the accusation I burned
you gently

Sometimes I Wonder Why It Has to Rain

maybe the clouds feel too dim in the caress of sunlight

maybe my grandmother is watering the earth
for she knows I let my irises choke on weeds

maybe raging fires are begging for forgiveness

maybe God wanted me
to remember the innocence it takes, outstretched
tongues to taste doom

maybe Niagara evaporates here to remind me
how insignificant I am
compared to falling water

maybe the sky offers to mourn for me

        because these tear ducts river
        their way into a desert

        and I find myself wishing I could
        know why these panes I sit between
        are just a little harder than the pains
        felt every time I catch myself

        tap tap tapping my cheek
        against the unforgiving glass searching for
        the rainbow between the hail

        tap tap tapping against the seeping
        cracks in torn-papered walls
        tapping their way through locked doors and flooding
        this room

maybe the earth just needed a change of pace

Photograph Behind the Lids

I want to be tall grass that mirrors
the green in someone else's
eyes, among flowers bathing
in the sunlight
that returns with every sunrise

bur I am starlight
that paints the flowers black
against the sky, despite my best
effort to portray them alive

Thirst

my throat is made of sand paper
the water that scratches its way
down doesn't replenish anything

it'll be as empty as Lake Erie
if you take our sunken ships and liquid
and horizons and memory

I spend so long trying to evaporate
you from me, there is
nothing to let go

I spend so long evaporating
myself from emotion, I can't
get my tear ducts to let go

these eyes are made of sand paper
lubricating them
doesn't replenish me

I'll feel as empty as Lake Erie
if I take out you and hope
and tears and memory

Illusion

if this cliff that holds up falling water
        decides to crumble
                do you think we'll fall into the gorge

or will we believe
        for a second
                we are birds learning how to fly

Practicing Darkness

I crawl out of this reassuring bed and let myself succumb to my eyelids, my fingers grasp empty air until they secure themselves to the wall, I let my feet stumble over the shoes on the floor and bruise my shins against the side of the door, find the bathroom light switch, and only let my fingers graze it, I fumble for the faucet, set my finger in the glass I nearly knock to the floor and wait for the water to nudge the tips before I place the glass to my lips.

I suppose I could just open my eyes and find my way to the sink in half the time, but it's the hopelessness, not the water, that draws me in.

Three

Night Raid

you make these sockets
a battlefield and set your
function to self-destruct

strip skin of color, so this
bloodshed turns an iris-covered
field into hopelessness

build a wall of haze that I try
to slice down with plastic
but you find a way to rebuild

I don't know how much longer I can
help you from my side. you abandon
the shield, shredding this tissue to pieces

a dried-out duct can't river its way into
washing out the wounded, and
medication will only ease the pain

        bombs are closing in
        and in this hour of need
        all I ask of you is one thing

            brace
            for impact

            guard yourself
            from your weapons

            if we don't call
            a cease fire

            we'll both be
            blind to sunrises

When I Admitted I Didn't Want to Move Fast

I run to the
moonlit shore, as I dip
in the shivering river
your voice still lures me in

>   *I don't*
>   *want to*
>   *sift*

into this rhythmic motion
where I try to pull for you
and you try to pull for me
in this rhythmic motion

>   *I don't*
>   *want*
>   *to sink*

beneath the weight of Niagara pressing
deeply into skin, where I can't find my way up
and you keep dragging me in

>   *and I don't want*
>   *to swallow a mouth*
>   *of rocks*

but truth buries itself in
this gorge until my words
are grounded and I can't
taste you in my teeth

The Belief of Fictitious Doubts

at what point did I realize that even the moon
doesn't always appear fully stable, even when it is

and despite the miles between us, when did we become
old enough to know that we no longer question

why it only appears to us
when we truly lose our minds

when did we start blaming Peter Pan for slipping
slivers of light into our darkest ignorance

or giving us the courage to be
the monsters underneath our mattresses

You Wish on Lanterns, I Wish to Be a Lantern

maybe I was never strong enough
to carry fire in my eyes

like forgotten August dusk unable to
hold a dying horizon

sometimes I still wish I could be the emeralds
wisping their way through parched grass

I wish I could hold bioluminescence
like we did in the summer of '99

when we collected mason jars to fill
with embers pulled from the sky

but just like that summer, we faded
into echoes of released fire

just like you faded and I stopped
trying to capture green in my eyes

In This Mirror

I hate my reflection
I hate these blemishes
I can't even look at them

somewhere, there's a reflection
that cant hold on to a girl

Mirror In This

eye hate my reflection
eye hate these blemishes
eye can't even look at them

somewhere there's a girl
that can't hold on to a reflection

To Be a Beast is to Be a Self

they tell her she can't be
like them because she spends too long
hiding behind the fog instead of sitting
among irises in the fields

she's too afraid to open her eyes and find
all the flowers have died like she dies
every time she sees the beast looking
back at her in the mirror

she wants to rip it with her claws, leave
graffiti on the glass, but she rips out her
eyes and replaces them with glass so
the mirror can only ever reflect itself

now when she goes to open her eyes in
the field, the irises will be left alone to die
but she'll never know because the fog
can only ever reflect itself

Spreading Ashes

this is what I get
(isn't it)

for believing in you
the way you believed in the stars (I couldn't see)

I knew (all along) I was only sticking my hands
in flames when I reached (for you)

now I sit in this rubble and trace words for you
and I don't know if it's promises you wrote me
or my uncertain poetry

my hands are so filthy, I can't write anymore

I'll let these words dry up and return to former glory
(ash or dust or something in between)

I'll wipe these memories from my hands
collect them in a bottle and ship them off to sea
so they can exist, or wish on stars, or (hopefully) sink

Plunging Vessels

We talk on the phone until 2:20 AM. You end the conversation by saying you will never let go. You insist we are strong enough to never leave each other stranded in the Atlantic.

But hours have now passed and there aren't enough flashlights to find me in this body of sea and in this sea of bodies. I'm grown tired of searching for a flare, or the lingering smoke of one. There are barriers of ice that can't echo my voice. I cling to drift wood with frostbitten fingers. The horizon is lifeless and the water is colorless. These lips are colorless and I am lifeless. I have become a silence made of silence that's everything but too quiet, left to drift with the shattered plates that no one will ever notice are missing.

X

this is where you bury me

nestled beneath trinkets
wedged in a box
of rehearsed lines and faith

built on sand, that runs between
my toes like water through body
(almost) purifying me

I can only imagine (how water
could) glisten off a horizon

like I, beneath this beach
can almost glisten
in my bloodstream

I'm marked with an indentation
that creases like blades in my forehead
coded in red (and meant) for expiration

I trace these lines I trace these lines
I trace these again and again I trace

I don't know what I'm looking for
but maybe if I try these lines hard enough
I'll dig my way out of this gold

I Am a Neap Tide

bioluminescence is most
noticeable five days
after the moon is full

it's only then that the waves begin
to miss the protection of light

I long to find protection in light

but this pupil like a waning
gibbous must have always
been destined for darkness

Don't—Come Find Me

This is the place where mice are not uninvited as pests and heartbroken coyotes are allowed to openly grieve. This is the place where fire is allowed to blaze until it burns itself out. This is the place where I solitude myself behind dry book pages and cracked coffee mugs, where my hand introduces itself to the pen, and the pen introduces itself to the leaves. This is the place where I submerge myself beside lake water that only mirrors a dissipating sun until the fog slips in, and the lake forgets how to reflect.

Four

Perceiving Obscurity

I run

with the dark horses
through the dead of light

so all they can see
is the camouflage of us
in silhouettes of dresses

I run

because I am a dark horse
against this dying horizon

and all I can see
is the camouflage of us
wearing dresses of silhouettes

Storm-gazing

I only look for heat lightning
when I'm tangled
with metal
on the front porch

and every time it hails, I'm foolish
enough to stretch my hand
only far enough to watch it
indent my skin

Afterglow

ember is the last chance for the fire
to prove itself, a last resort

like I resort to trusting the distance
of stars more than I trust this moon

ember is the fire's last hope, smoldering
through the only remaining log, so slowly

so beautifully, like the fireflies that used to
crystal here

ember is the fire's final prayer for one
last gust of a forgiving wind

I don't know how to forgive myself
for letting you smother me

ember is the last ounce of protection before
the wolves close in

I am closing
in

as the smoke cuts through
and negotiates for the flame

Fuse

I let you dissipate with the last
of the poems that I shredded into
the log remains, not burned
but singed, left there

I no longer want to be
responsible for you, for the words
you etched into my brain, that I
in turn, etched with my pen

I try to rewrite myself, without
you, but instead I become
you. for I slip into
the ash as well

and now I am
responsible for me, burned
not singed, and wanting
to be left here

Nocturnal

I settle for the night. no matter
how hard I try, I just can't
seem to keep it
away. I settle
for the shadows
in the forest, that's what all
the wolves do. I practice
stealthy footsteps and listen
for the silence
I take to the silence
it's the only thing
that doesn't criticize me
I wait for the leaves
to gather in the trees here
in the dark, they convince
each other they are all
the same. I search for answers
for the river that flows to
somewhere, I need to find

I trust the night because the morning
seems to have forgotten me

Castaway

if the ripples in a pond are created
by a sinking
stone

can I

a stone
in this sinking
pond, be a ripple

Bordering

The air smells a little bit like the ocean and when the water sprays against your lips it feels just as cold only it doesn't taste as salty. When you stand on the edge and hear the thunder falling to the gorge you've forgotten how to listen for anything but the water calling. You cling to the metal railing and know it's the only thing that keeps you, too, from falling. The seagulls search for food and even if you don't have any you can still hear them behind you. People are gawking all around you, whispering about the rocks and the white caps and the mist. Your body sways like the rush of the current though you don't know where you're headed at all. You take a deep breath, feeling the wind seep its way into your chest.

You don't have to see Niagara Falls to know it exists.

6 A.M.

wake up to watch the sun slip light beneath the vapor

wake up for the piece of morning that clings to gloom

wake up like twilight wakes the stars

wake up before cars are asked to release the frost

wake up so loneliness can escape the roads

wake up before echoes become shy

wake up before birds give their wild permission to be free

Somewhere Between the Dew and 10 AM

I love the fog because it
camouflages itself when it tries
to overthrow the night
but it forces the morning rush to be
blind even with its headlights

it forces open signs to be invisible
until it's right before your eyes, it forces
traffic stops to tempt fate like I do
every time I cross a street, it
forces the sun to hide and it does
so while putting clouds to shame

I love the fog because it
forces the world to see
itself through a new set
of lenses, the way a curious
eye needs a clean bathroom
mirror to observe its naked
body after scrubbing itself
from the day's grime

I love the fog because I don't
need any mirror to erase
grime like I don't need the fog
to erase roads from
freshly-paved yellow

I love the fog because it leaves
me alone

End Notes

1. Zapruder, Matthew. *Why Poetry*. HarperCollins Publishers. New York, NY. 2017.

2. Nilsen, Emily. *Otolith*. Icehouse Poetry, an imprint of Goose Lane Editions, 2017.

3. Christie, Heather. *The Crying Book*. Catapult; Illustrated edition. November 5, 2019.

Acknowledgments

I would, first and foremost, like to thank God for blessing me with the challenges that have made me the person I am today. I used to think those challenges were the things that held me back, the things that defined me. Now, I know that they are the things that push me forward.

I'd like to thank my family: My parents, Daniel, Dell, Katie, Molly, Vinnie, Michelle, and everyone who has played a role in supporting and encouraging me in my journey. I'd list every single one of you, but we all know our family tree is a book.

I'd like to thank those in the blind community, who have been a guidance for me in this world, who really opened my eyes to a world of darkness and inspired me to work through it every day. People from the blind community and some of the alumni from the Michigan School for the Blind that have become family: Dianne Devereaux, Lucy Edmonds, Larry Posont, Fred and George Wurtzel, Gary and Vicki Kitts, as well as Gary and Lori Parobek. The counselors and campers at Camp Tusmeheta that gave me a look into this world in a way I had never seen before. Thank you to my best friend, Chelsea Henrizi, who has guided me through every light and dark place I have encountered.

Thank you to everyone at Finishing Line Press, who helped put this piece together, and gave it a home.

Thank you to Joze Groselj. for taking the time to create the beautiful artwork for the cover of this book.

And most of all, I'd like to thank everyone in the MFA program at New England College, without whom I would not be here. Thank you to the students, and the mentors for all the time and effort in helping me create the work that is in this collection. All the time put in to workshops and readings. I will forever be grateful for the endless support and guidance of that community. Thank you Jennifer Militello, Paige Ackerson-Kiely, Allison Titus, David Ryan, Tim Learde, and Chen Chen for being my guidance and motivation through the process of this book.

And a special thank you to Maura MacNeil and Andrew Morgan, for not only supporting and helping me on this piece as well but guiding me to strive beyond all my limits. I never would have found the courage to push myself as a writer without you.

Rebecca Kositzke was born and raised in Lansing, Michigan. She began writing stories in the sixth grade, when she attended Emanuel Lutheran School. From the first time she took a pen to paper, she knew that writing was something she wanted to continue doing for the rest of her life.

At the age of twenty, she spent a year attending Lansing Community College, where she took theater classes, and participated in the productions of *Almost Maine* and *Wind in the Willows*. This provided a further dive into the art of storytelling.

After taking some personal time off of school, she relocated to the small town of Henniker, New Hampshire, where she attended New England College, receiving her Bachelor of Fine Arts in Creative Writing. While attending, Kositzke placed all of her time and effort into engaging her writing skills with the community. She wrote for the school paper, *The NewEnglander*, creating book reviews for the physical and online platform. She became an Editor for the literary journal, *The Henniker Review*. After a year, Kositzke took on the role of Editor in Chief, guiding the book through its submission and publication process. Her nonfiction pieces, *Pure Michigan* and *Strangers* can be found in the 2017 edition, as well as a couple photographs taken in Kona, Hawaii.

In 2018, her first children's book, *Blaze of Glory*, was published through Page Publishing. From there, Kositzke went on to receive her Master of Fine Arts in Creative Writing with a focus in Poetry, from New England College. This provided the opportunity to engage with a community of writers, and continue advancing her writing skills, as well as her love for poetry.

Since then, Kositzke has worked as a childcare provider in Lansing, Michigan. She worked at Emanuel First Lutheran Church, as well as AppleTree and Gilden Woods Early Care and Preschool. Alongside teaching children, she has continued to engage in writing, taking any time she can to continue pursuing the words on the page.

www.ingramcontent.com/pod-product-compliance
Lightning Source LLC
Chambersburg PA
CBHW030057170426
43197CB00010B/1568